R.I.O.T.

Devotional

"Righteous Truths That Will Invade Your Life" — Vol. 2

Carman Ministries

Albury Publishing
P. O. Box 470406
Tulsa, Oklahoma 74147-0406

R.I.O.T. Devotional..."Righteous Truths That Will Invade Your Life" — Vol. 2
ISBN 1-88008-939-4
Copyright © 1995 by Carman Ministries
P.O. Box 5093
Brentwood, TN 37024-5093

Published by ALBURY PUBLISHING
P.O. Box 470406
Tulsa, Oklahoma 74147-0406

Contents

R.I.O.T. DEVOTIONAL — Volume 2

For many years, Carman Ministries has reached out to thousands of people around the world. As a result, many have been encouraged and many have come to Christ. Maybe you are one of them. But what happens when the concert is over and the devil is ready to catch you unsteady to trap you unaware? What are you gonna do when he launches one of his trials through your friends with BIG smiles to draw you into sin? Simple. You stop putting up with it. You stop being quiet. You get into God's Word...and you start a RIOT!

Welcome to the Carman Ministries daily devotional book that will enable you to start a R.I.O.T. (Righteous Invasion Of Truth) in your life and neighborhood. These daily power bites will not only give you the strength needed to destroy the works of the devil, they will also lead you into a deeper understanding of God's Word. This devotional, R.I.O.T. Volume II, is based on the last five songs on Carman's R.I.O.T. CD:

7 WAYS 2 PRAISE
STEP OF FAITH
NOT 4 SALE
THERE IS A GOD
AMEN

In this devotional you will:
- discover how to praise God in spite of circumstances;
- worship God the Bible way;
- walk in strong faith;
- pray with power;
- withstand the devil's compromise;
- learn to start a RIOT!;
- develop a deeper understanding of Jesus' ministry;
- experience a deeper touch of the Holy Spirit;
- discover God's magnificent works in Creation;
- and much, much more!

To get the most out of this devo book:
- Listen to the CD song before reading each devo.
- Pray for the Holy Spirit to teach and guide you.
- Have your Bible open and read every Scripture referred to each day.
- Act on the RIOT ACT each day.
- Put God's Word and truth in your heart.
- Share what you learn about Jesus from this devo book with others.

Go for it. There's no way we're gonna leave here quiet. Come on y'all, let's start a R.I.O.T.!

7 Ways To Worship

Way back in the Bible, the Hebrew language says
That we were taught that we would
praise the Lord in seven ways
Seven great expressions, seven different flows
Seven ways to worship God and this is how it goes

JESUS SAID TO HIM, "AWAY FROM ME, SATAN! FOR IT IS WRITTEN: 'WORSHIP THE LORD YOUR GOD, AND SERVE HIM ONLY.'" (MATTHEW 4:10)

R. I. O. T. —RIGHTEOUS INVASION OF TRUTH

So what is worship? Let me give you a clue:
    It starts with God, not me or you!
Worship doesn't focus on you or me,
    We come in praise on bended knee.
It's for an audience of One—
    The Father, the Spirit and the Son!
It can't be fake and here's the proof,
    You worship the Lord in spirit and truth!

Get the picture? Ever walk out of a worship service and say, "Man, that was a bummer. Dull. Boooring!" But what did you bring to worship? You see, worship doesn't happen to impress you. In worship we bring the sacrifice of ourselves into the presence of God. We come to praise Him. Not the preacher, the choir or the Sunday School teacher. We come to praise Him!

So what should you *get* out of worship? Buzzzz! Wrong question. The question should be, "What should you *bring* to worship?" Will you bring your praise, your reverence, your awe, your offerings, your whole self? Do it now, get off of the shelf!

So get ready to worship. Don't come seeking His gifts, seek God the Giver. Don't come to get. Come to give. In giving, you will receive.

R.I.O.T. ACT

"God is Spirit, and his worshipers must worship in spirit and in truth." (John 4:24)

Hold on, get ready. Don't sit there on your hands looking "dignified" and steady. Get up on your feet, start to move to His beat. Get your hands and voice raised for these 7 ways 2 praise.

Praising God In Spite Of...

Number one is towdah (towdah), It's the sacrifice
Praising God in spite the fact your
world is in a vice
It's praise that pushes through the
wall of all adversity
An offering that flows to heaven in our time of need

THROUGH JESUS, THEREFORE, LET US CONTINUALLY OFFER TO GOD A SACRIFICE OF PRAISE—THE FRUIT OF LIPS THAT CONFESS HIS NAME. (HEBREWS 13:15)

R.I.O.T.—RIGHTEOUS INVASION OF TRUTH

My day was the worst! Late to work after school. Forgot my money for lunch. Saw someone wearing the exact same shirt as me. Had a fight with my best friend. And you say, "Praise the Lord!?" It's great praising God when things are great. But praising Him in everything? Right! Give me a break!

How do you offer the sacrifice of praise to God when your day is rotten and you feel terrible? Simple. Don't praise God for the problem. Praise God in spite of the problem. Praise Him through the problem. Satan gets smashed every time God gets glory instead of grumbling. Plug into God's power with praise. Praise Him before He meets your need.

So, you think God doesn't care about your circumstance? Of course He does! But He cares first and foremost about you and your response. With a response of faith and praise from you, God will work miracles in spite of your circumstances. So don't pray, "God change that!" Instead pray, "God, change me!" Changed, we can confront and overcome every circumstance. Be an overcomer, not a victim! Instead of being sour and depressed about your problems, offer up praise to Him no matter what the situation.

R.I.O.T. ACT

Offer the sacrifice of praise! *"I will praise you, O Lord, with all my heart!"* (Psalm 9:1)

Troubled? Confused? Anxious? Depressed? Instead of burning up, come into God's rest.

Mind, Body, Spirit— Praise the Lord!

Somebody say mind (mind)
Praise the Lord (praise the Lord)
Say body (body)
Praise the Lord (praise the Lord)
Spirit (Spirit)
Praise the Lord (praise the Lord)

LET EVERYTHING THAT HAS BREATH PRAISE THE LORD. PRAISE THE LORD. (PSALM 150:6)

R.I.O.T.—RIGHTEOUS INVASION OF TRUTH

Mind—Let's praise, praise the Lord! Every thought can praise the Lord. Each word in every thought can give God praise. So focus your mind. Center your thoughts. Set your mind on Jesus and let it go!

Selfish thoughts, GO!
Dumb thoughts, GO!
Angry thoughts, GO!
Depressed thoughts, GO!

Aimless thoughts, GO!
Dirty thoughts, GO!
Perverted thoughts, GO!
Confused thoughts, GO!

"...And we take captive every thought to make it obedient to Christ." (2 Corinthians 10:5)

Body—Let's praise, praise the Lord! Raise those hands. Clap them too. Shout and dance. Got the clue? What's-a-matter, body, stuck to the pew with glue?

Hands, CLAP!
Body, MOVE!

10

Voice, SING!
Ears, HEAR!
Lips, PRAISE!

Feet, DANCE!
Tongue, SHOUT!
Arms, UP and OUT!

"Sing to the Lord a new song, his praise in the assembly of the saints...Praise him with tambourine and dancing...Clap your hands, all you nations; shout to God with cries of joy." (Psalm 149:1; 150:4; 47:1)

Spirit—Let's praise, praise the Lord! Out of the depths of your being, praise and worship Him. Let your spirit pray, worship and sing.

Spirit, PRAY!
Spirit, SING!
Spirit, ADORE!
Praise the Lord for everything!

Spirit, SEEK!
Spirit, REJOICE!
Spirit, speak in God's voice!

"God is Spirit, and his worshipers must worship in spirit and in truth." (John 4:24)

R.I.O.T. ACT

"Let the name of the Lord be praised, both now and forevermore. From the rising of the sun to the place where it sets, the name of the Lord is to be praised." (Psalm 113:2-3)

Hey you! Yeah, I mean you—all of you. Praise the Lord!

Lift Your Hands

*Number two's yadah (yadah), that means lift
your hands
In response to what the Lord has done throughout
the land
An outward sign of what's inside for all the
world to see
A demonstration of our love so come praise
the Lord with me*

**I WILL PRAISE YOU AS LONG AS I LIVE, AND
IN YOUR NAME I WILL LIFT UP MY HANDS.
(PSALM 63:4)**

R.I.O.T.—RIGHTEOUS INVASION OF TRUTH

In first grade, Jamie and Sarah were taught to
raise their hands if... well, if they had a question or
an answer. Or if they needed to leave the room to
be excused. Then at camp that summer, they were
taught to raise their hands and shut their mouths.
So what's so strange about worship? What's the
deal about it that so many get nervous about?
When I raise my hands I don't have a question or
an answer and don't have an excuse to leave the
room. So, uplifted hands in worship, what do they
mean?

What about, "Hi ya', Dad, just wavin' to you."
How about, "Love You, Jesus, just love You true!"
What about, "Welcome, Spirit, welcome to You!" How
about, "Father, I adore You, Son and Spirit, too."

Your heavenly Father is just waiting for you. He is waiting to spend time with, talk with, and listen to you. Your heavenly Father, wants to pick you up just like a dad would. He wants to sit you on His lap, hug you and talk with you face to face. So stretch out your hands and reach up to Him, saying, "Daddy, pick me up, lift me into Your grace!"

R.I.O.T. ACT

Lift your hands to heaven and put your hands in His. *"Lift up your hands in the sanctuary and praise the Lord."* (Psalm 134:2)

Give God a gift—give your arms a lift.

Clap Those Hands!

*Can you wave one hand and say praise the Lord
(praise the Lord)
Can you wave both hands and say praise the Lord
(praise the Lord)
Now can you clap those hands and say praise the
Lord (praise the Lord)*

**CLAP YOUR HANDS, ALL YOU NATIONS;
SHOUT TO GOD WITH CRIES OF JOY.
(PSALM 47:1)**

R.I.O.T.—RIGHTEOUS INVASION OF TRUTH

So, who likes applause? Guess everyone does, don't they? Actors after a great play love a standing ovation. Singers after a great performance love applause. Sports teams after a great game relish cheers and clapping. Speakers after a rousing message enjoy thunderous applause. Many bow and curtsy, wave and smile when they receive it. Don't they?

So why do we clap our hands before the Lord? Does He need it? Could it be that God enjoys it? Has He created everything we can see for our standing ovation? No way. God is above mere human vanity. He doesn't need it. But we need to give it. You see, we have this tendency to give ourselves credit where credit isn't due. We didn't create ourselves. He did! We can't paint a sunset. God does it every day! We didn't invent music. The

Lord did! We can't perform miracles. He does! Because of His grace!

So when you see a delicate, finely crafted, beautiful flower, clap your hands—to God. Next time you spy an awesome sunrise or sunset, give God a standing ovation! When your eyes behold beauty or your ears hear the music of birds or a splashing, laughing stream—loudly applaud and cheer the Lord!

If you're willing to give all those people performances a rousing ovation, then how much more should you be willing to get on your feet and clap for the Lord!

R.I.O.T. ACT

"For you, O Lord, are the Most High over all the earth; you are exalted far above all gods." (Psalm 97:9)

Don't hold back. Cut no slack. Put your hands together—go ahead, clap!

Bow In His Presence

*Number three is baruch (baw•rook), that simply
means to bow
In the awesome presence of the Lord and
all His power
Just be overwhelmed 'cause you hardly can believe
That you've been given favor by His Holy Majesty*

**COME, LET US BOW DOWN IN WORSHIP,
LET US KNEEL BEFORE THE LORD OUR
MAKER; FOR HE IS OUR GOD AND WE ARE
THE PEOPLE OF HIS PASTURE, THE FLOCK
UNDER HIS CARE. (PSALM 95:6-7)**

R.I.O.T.—RIGHTEOUS INVASION OF TRUTH

The King was throwing a party. He wanted
everyone there. Out went the invites, but only
came a few—leaving room to spare. Sad day for
the King? Don't say! If those invited wouldn't
come, then He'd find another way. *Go into the
streets. Invite all you see. The banquet is ready and
it's gonna be free.* The King's orders went out, and
to every street corner rushed His servants looking
for any who would be a comer.

So into the party rushed just anybody, good and
bad. What a motley looking crew, a little ragged
you might say. But whoever came got to stay.
Those who missed out were the ones who stayed
away. (You can read this story for yourself in
Matthew 22:1-14)

Now imagine yourself a beggar in rags looking for aluminum cans in trash bins and bags. When suddenly, a King spies you in the garbage heap. Over he comes, to invite you to a feast. Free food, free drinks, free clothes, no strings attached save one. You had to come.

You stand there staring, the King is there. Funny, as bad as you've been, all you feel is His care.

This is what Jesus did for you and me, when He gave His life to set us free!

R.I.O.T. ACT

"For many are invited, but few are chosen." *(Matthew 22:14)*

Bow before Jesus, bow before your King, humble yourself, He is everything!

PRAISE THE LORD!

Praise the Lord
Praise the Lord
Praise the Lord
Praise the Lord

PRAISE THE LORD, O MY SOUL, ALL MY INMOST BEING, PRAISE HIS HOLY NAME. PRAISE THE LORD, O MY SOUL, AND FORGET NOT ALL HIS BENEFITS. (PSALM 103:1-2)

R.I.O.T.—RIGHTEOUS INVASION OF TRUTH

So what if you don't feel like praising Him. Know what? If God never did anything else for you in your life, He has already done enough to be praised forever. *No kidding? For real! So, what's with this praise thing?* I'll tell you the deal.

(Read this and then stop. Close your eyes and see it.)

A cross.
   Not just any cross.
      The Man is on the cross.
         Not just any man—not a murderer,
            liar or thief.
An innocent man, bearing your grief.
   Why? What's He done?
      Nothin' 'cept lovin' you and me, that's
         right, He died for you on the tree.
Sin kept you away from the Father.
   So the Son died to bring you back home.

Couldn't go back home without the
Man on the cross,
Dying there all alone.

Picture that! Bleeding, hurting, scared and marred.

Thorns pushed into his head. Hanging
there, nearly dead.
His back whipped down to the bone.
Not a pretty picture—this marred and
bleeding one all alone.
But stop, it is a praise picture, see
it if you can.
Jesus hung on the cross to make you a
new man!

Now stop. Project that picture on the screen of your mind. What do you see? That's what God did to set you free. So, praise the Lord when you rise up and lie down. Praise Him in the bathroom. Get rid of that frown! Praise Him at church and when you're at home. Praise Him in a crowd and when you're all alone!

R.I.O.T. ACT

"Speak to one another with psalms, hymns and spiritual songs..." (Ephesians 5:19)

Put the devil in a daze—Give the Lord praise!

Shout!

*This fourth one is shabach (shabach), it is what we
call the shout
It's praise that's given way before the answer
comes about
A public testimony that drowns out all the noise
Of whiners and complainers as the saints all lift
their voice*

**WITH PRAISE AND THANKSGIVING THEY
SANG TO THE LORD: "HE IS GOOD; HIS
LOVE TO ISRAEL ENDURES FOREVER." AND
ALL THE PEOPLE GAVE A GREAT SHOUT OF
PRAISE TO THE LORD, BECAUSE THE FOUN-
DATION OF THE HOUSE OF THE LORD WAS
LAID. (EZRA 3:11)**

R.I.O.T.—RIGHTEOUS INVASION OF TRUTH

So, where do you shout the loudest? At a foot-
ball, basketball, volleyball, hockey or soccer game
when your team is playing? Or is it at a concert
when your favorite group is on stage? Could it be
that you shout the loudest in anger instead of in
praise? Or, are you a quiet person and feel embarrassed to make too much noise in public?

What if you shouted before the game begins,
the team's ahead or the concert is played? What if
you shouted before the answer came? What if you
praised God before the miracle or healing? What
if, while others were complaining, whining,

sniping and griping, you lifted your voice, and shouted God's praise?

Sure, it's easier to praise God when things are great. But notice the Bible text you just read. The people shouted their praise to the Lord—not when the Temple was finished—but when the starting foundation only had been laid. By faith they were shouting praise for what would be done as much as for what had already happened. Zounds! God honors that!

So start learning to shout your praise to God, even before the answer has come. Because of the cross and the resurrection, you know the victory has been won.

R.I.O.T. ACT

"When the trumpets sounded, the people shouted, and at the sound of the trumpet, when the people gave a loud shout, the wall collapsed; so every man charged straight in, and they took the city." (Joshua 6:20)

Feeling down? Face in a frown?
Give a shout. Your shout's
got clout!

Shout! (Part 2)

If you believe that God's alive, shout yeah (yeah)
If you believe that He's worthy of our praise, shout yeah (yeah)
If you believe the answer's on the way, shout yeah (yeah)

GOD HAS ASCENDED AMID SHOUTS OF JOY, THE LORD AMID THE SOUNDING OF TRUMPETS. SING PRAISES TO GOD, SING PRAISES; SING PRAISES TO OUR KING, SING PRAISES. (PSALM 47:5-6)

R.I.O.T.—RIGHTEOUS INVASION OF TRUTH

Barb went around telling everyone that God had healed her. Everyone knew she had cancer. Her test results were gloomy and the doctors were pessimistic about the effectiveness of any treatment. Still, Barb went around singing and thanking God for her healing. Some friends thought she had lost it. Others felt that she was denying reality. But most thought it was just a way to reassure and comfort herself.

What gave her the motivation to be so up in such a down situation? Could it be that she simply believed that the same Jesus who healed the sick 2,000 years ago was still alive? Could it be that Jesus was worthy of praise in spite of her circumstances? Could it be that faith gives rise to praise before we can clearly see the outcome of a situation? Could it be? Yes, it could! And yes, it should!

Next time you face a battle, spit victory into the face of the devil. Next time you're dealt a lousy hand, throw away the cards and refuse to play the game. Next time you've got a question without any answer in sight, believe the God of answers instead of Satan's world of fright. Instead of speaking doom and gloom, speak God's Word that defeats every temptation, attack and fearful doubt. Could it be that Barb was healed? Shout yeah! Yes it could. Believe, don't doubt!

R.I.O.T. ACT

"For no matter how many promises God has made, they are Yes' in Christ. And so through him the Amen' is spoken by us to the glory of God." (2 Corinthians 1:20)

No jive, God's alive. Shout, "YEAH!" today! He's alive!

Play The Instruments in Praise!

Number five is zamar (zamar), this one you'll like
for sure
It's playing any instrument that glorifies the Lord
Instruments that blast, instruments that strum
Instruments that keep the beat, so I'll praise Him
on my drum!

LET EVERYTHING THAT HAS BREATH PRAISE THE LORD. PRAISE THE LORD. (PSALM 150:6)

R.I.O.T. — RIGHTEOUS INVASION OF TRUTH

Praise the Lord.
Praise God in his sanctuary;
    praise him in his mighty heavens.
Praise him for his acts of power;
    praise him for his surpassing greatness.
Praise him with the sounding of the trumpet,
    praise him with the harp and lyre,
Praise him with tambourine and dancing,
    praise him with the strings and flute,
    praise him with the clash of cymbals,
    praise him with resounding cymbals.
Let everything that has breath praise the Lord.
Praise the Lord. (Psalm 150)

Nobody's lookin'. Think of your favorite instrument. What is it? Guitar? Drums? Keyboard? Trumpet? Flute? Cymbals? Whatever. Make like that instrument right now. That's right. Pretend you are that instrument. Play it. Make the noises and sounds it makes. Bop around your room making praise with that instrument at the top of your lungs. Ain't it great? Praise the Lord!

Be an orchestra. Be a band. Be anything but silent. Make like a music stand. Jesus says if you're silent the rocks will cry out with praise. So don't be outdone by a crummy rock. Be or play an instrument. Come on, let's rock!

R.I.O.T. ACT

Be a full orchestra. Be every instrument of praise. *"Shout with joy to God, all the earth! Sing the glory of his name; make his praise glorious!"* *(Psalm 66:1,2)*

Strike up the band, we're gonna slam, lift your heart to God, come on let's jam!

Rave and Boast About the Lord

*Six we call halal (haw•lal) that means to rave
and boast
And praise the Lord in such a way that gets you
on your toes
(Wait a minute, wait a minute) What (hey, now,
what did you say), it's beyond just clappin hands
but best of all, this is the one that makes you
wanna dance*

PRAISE HIM WITH TAMBOURINE AND DANCING. (PSALM 150:4)

R.I.O.T.—RIGHTEOUS INVASION OF TRUTH

Proper praise...I say there ole chap, what would you think that might be? Proper praise simply is not politely clapping hands. Proper praise certainly isn't being dignified. Proper praise doesn't always do what's "proper" in other's eyes.

So, Yo, what's proper? That which comes from the heart! That's right! It's that which is set apart just for Jesus without gettin' uptight. That which stirs up our spirit and emotions toward Him. If you want to be completely proper, start to rave about Him.

Rave about His love and power,
    Rave about His might,

Rave about His mercy,
　　Rave about His light.

Rave about His miracles,
　　Rave about His cross,
　　　　Rave about His resurrection,
　　　　　　And praise Him 'cause He's boss.

Now get up on your toes,
　　And reach for the heavens,
　　　　Reach up to Jesus,
　　　　　　For visiting us from heaven.

Now get to clappin' and do some dancin',
　　Dance in the round,
　　　　Dance in a line,
　　　　　　Go ahead, dance up and down.

Call it hallel,
　　Gettin' loud,
　　　　Giving praise to Jesus in a crowd!

R.I.O.T. ACT

Rave and crave to be in the presence of Jesus.
"...Again you will take up your tambourines and go out to dance with the joyful." (Jeremiah 31:4)

. . . .

Holdin' back? Get on track! Shout your hallelujah—Don't hold back!

. . . .

Do it all—Rejoice Before the Lord!

Finally, tehillah (tehiliah), seven is the best
It's the one that is the combination of the rest
It's singing and it's shouting, it's dancing and
it's more
It's wild, it's fun so everyone rejoice before the Lord!

REJOICE IN THE LORD ALWAYS. I WILL SAY IT AGAIN: REJOICE! (PHILIPPIANS 4:4)

R.I.O.T.—RIGHTEOUS INVASION OF TRUTH

Praise isn't just doing certain things like clapping, dancing, singing, shouting, or playing instruments. Praise can be doing everything in our life to honor God as we do it our very best. In fact, praise can be so extravagant that others may even be critical of it.

Like Mary, the sister of Martha. She owned an extravagant bottle of perfume. As a dinner was being served in Jesus' honor, she reached for her expensive bottle and moved toward Jesus. A hush came over the room. Perhaps she would dab a bit on His forehead to honor Him. Perhaps she would pour a bit on His head to anoint Him. Or perhaps she would give it as a gift to Him to use as He wished. After all, one disciple thought, it could be sold and the money given to the poor. But she didn't use her perfume for any of these things.

Good grief! Not that! Mary emptied the contents of that priceless perfume on Jesus' feet. How wasteful! How extravagant! Why do such a thing? Then she wiped His feet with her hair! How disgusting! How indiscreet! (You can read this story in John 12:1-10)

Extravagant, unbounded, unlimited, unconditional love for Jesus compelled Mary to anoint Jesus. That's what tehiliah is all about—abundant, unlimited, boundless praise that gives everything we can—come on, shout!

R.I.O.T. ACT

"...I will celebrate before the Lord."
(2 Samuel 6:21)

Make the right choice and lift up your voice—it's time to rejoice!

Seed of Faith

Above the noise I hear the voice
Of God givin' the choice for me to say
I do believe and will receive
Within the heart of me the seed of faith

OTHERS, LIKE SEED SOWN ON GOOD SOIL, HEAR THE WORD, ACCEPT IT, AND PRODUCE A CROP—THIRTY, SIXTY OR EVEN A HUNDRED TIMES WHAT WAS SOWN. (MARK 4:20)

R.I.O.T.—RIGHTEOUS INVASION OF TRUTH

A farmer goes out to sow seed. Some of the seed falls on the path where the birds come and snatch it away. Other seed lands on rocky soil where it springs up quickly, with only shallow roots. As the sun beats down on it, it withers and dies. Other seed falls among thorns. As it grows, the thorns surround and choke it. Still other seed lands on good soil and produces a crop multiplying itself many times over. (See Mark 4:1-20)

What kind of soil is your heart? The seed is God's Word. The soil is your heart. Do you have a heart to receive God's Word? Are you willing to be the soil of faith that gives birth to a new creation in Jesus Christ? *"Therefore, if anyone is in Christ, he is a new creation; the old has gone, the new has come!"* (2 Corinthians 5:17)

To each of us comes a choice when we hear

the call of Christ, "Come, follow Me." If our hearts are hard, His Word is simply snatched away by the enemy.

But if we soften our hearts and hear His voice, the Word of God takes good root in our lives. We believe and receive, trust and obey, and God blesses us the Bible way!

R.I.O.T. ACT

"That if you confess with your mouth, 'Jesus is Lord,' and believe in your heart that God raised him from the dead, you will be saved." *(Romans 10:9)*

Soften your heart. Turn from the old way. Trust God's Word. Jesus is the way.

Baby Steps

He does accept a baby step
As long as I have kept His word inside

A MAN'S STEPS ARE DIRECTED BY THE LORD. (PROVERBS 20:24)

R.I.O.T.—RIGHTEOUS INVASION OF TRUTH

Try this. Close your eyes or blindfold yourself. Then walk around your room. Hard? Sort of. But since you've been in your room for a while, you know where most of the stuff is so you can find your way. But what if you were in a brand new place and had never been there before? And what if you were blindfolded? It would be nearly impossible to find your way then. But what if in your new place, even though you were blindfolded, you had a friend who was willing to lead you around the room? If you took his hand, trusted him and walked where he told you to walk, then you could find your way.

And what about being born? I mean physically. Had you ever been born before? Nah, physical birth ushers everyone into a new world. Sure, your eyes are opened, but it's still like walking blind because you've never been here before. The same is true when you're born again. When you are born spiritually as a new creation in Jesus Christ, you have never been His way before. But Jesus is that friend in the room who will lead you around as you grow.

He knows where to go, how to avoid the pitfalls and where peace and joy can be found.

After a while, your confidence will grow, not so much in yourself, but in Jesus. As you learn to trust Him you'll be ready to help others find their way. And the journey is worth it, 'cause its destination is His Throne.

R.I.O.T. ACT

"...we will in all things grow up into him who is the Head...." (Ephesians 4:15)

To walk the talk is the only choice—I need is to hear and trust His voice.

Go Ahead and Try

But Jesus knows that I must grow
And tells me I must go ahead and try
Well all right, okay, I guess it's up, up and away

INSTEAD, SPEAKING THE TRUTH IN LOVE, WE WILL IN ALL THINGS GROW UP INTO HIM WHO IS THE HEAD, THAT IS, CHRIST. (EPHESIANS 4:15)

R.I.O.T.—RIGHTEOUS INVASION OF TRUTH

Watch a baby take her first steps. At first, she pulls up on things—tables, chairs, anything she can hold onto. Then she walks around those things. Slowly at first, then with more confidence. Sure there are falls, but that's to be expected. Finally, she tries something new. Now she is going to walk away from the chair all by herself. She can be coaxed into a few steps by Mom or Dad. Smiling and giggling she pushes away and runs, falling into her parent's arms.

The same is true for faith. As new babies in Christ, walking in the Spirit does not come naturally. We have to crawl before we pull up; we have to pull up before we step out; and we have to step out with a step or two before we walk. It's all part of growing up.

There is no such thing as an instant Christian. Can't microwave faith or stir fry obedience. This growing up in Christ takes time.

Think about it. It's hard to pray for cancer to be healed if you haven't first believed for a headache. It's hard to trust God with your finances if you haven't first trusted Him with an offering. It's hard to go overseas as a missionary until you've first tried to witness to someone at school or next door. So start with the small things, and watch your faith grow!

R.I.O.T. ACT

Take one step. The next step He has shown you. Just be obedient. *"If you are willing and obedient, you will eat the best from the land."* (Isaiah 1:19)

He knows you must grow. Don't rush, just keep on the go!

Walkin' Out on God's Promises

I'm takin' a step, takin' a step of faith
Walkin' out on the promises God made
Takin' a giant leap in the air
Steppin' out on nothin' and findin' somethin' there
Tellin' the doubt to wait, wait, wait, wait, wait
I'm takin' a step of faith

JESUS REPLIED, "I TELL YOU THE TRUTH, IF YOU HAVE FAITH AND DO NOT DOUBT, NOT ONLY CAN YOU DO WHAT WAS DONE TO THE FIG TREE, BUT ALSO YOU CAN SAY TO THIS MOUNTAIN, 'GO, THROW YOURSELF INTO THE SEA,' AND IT WILL BE DONE. IF YOU BELIEVE, YOU WILL RECEIVE WHATEVER YOU ASK IN PRAYER."
(MATTHEW 21:21-22)

R.I.O.T.—RIGHTEOUS INVASION OF TRUTH

Jennifer's parents had gotten a divorce. She couldn't believe it. They both said they loved her, but that wasn't enough to keep them together. So splitting up everything, they went their separate ways. Since Jennifer was fifteen, they let her decide who she would live with. The choice seemed easy. Mom was keeping the house. And, Jennifer and her Mom got along pretty well. So, she stayed put.

On the other hand, Jennifer had always had a good relationship with her dad. But one missed time together turned into two, then five and then more. So Jennifer prayed, "Father God, I don't know why mom and dad quit loving one another. But I do know they still love me. So I ask You in Jesus' name that You would help dad to keep his promises in visiting me."

Now be careful. God's promises don't always happen the way we expect or in the timing we want. God never forces His will on anyone. But when we pray His will He can convict others toward a change in heart. So always believe, step out in faith and love. What about Jennifer's dad? He called to apologize the next week.

R.I.O.T. ACT

"[Love] *bears all things, believes all things, hopes all things, endures all things.*" (1 Corinthians 13:7 NKJV)

I'm steppin' out in faith, not moved by what I see, I'm tell'n doubt to walk—I'm takin' the leap.

What To Do With Doubt

It turns me out to think I'd doubt
Someone with so much clout from up above

BUT WHEN HE ASKS, HE MUST BELIEVE AND NOT DOUBT, BECAUSE HE WHO DOUBTS IS LIKE A WAVE OF THE SEA, BLOWN AND TOSSED BY THE WIND. (JAMES 1:6)

R.I.O.T.—RIGHTEOUS INVASION OF TRUTH

There is what doubt is,
>And there is what doubt ain't.

First, what it ain't...
>Doubt ain't questions asked honest and fairly,
>God's not threatened, His truth lines up squarely.

Doubt ain't thoughts wondering what it's all about,

God don't mind if you yell, scream or shout.
>Doubt ain't hurt when disappointed or scared,
>God don't back down even when He's dared.

Doubt ain't the pain when you feel real drained,

God's always there, He's always the same.

Now, let's take a look at what doubt is all about...

Doubt is questioning whether God's a
    liar,
But God never fibs, He never gets
    caught in a mire.
Doubt is attacking God's integrity,
But God's always truth—and I don't mean
    maybe.
Doubt is believing Satan's lie,
But God can be trusted—He cannot
    lie.
So stop worrying about questions, wondering
and searching out what's new,
    He's not out to get you 'cause you
    have a question or two.
When ya can't see God's hand, know what
He's about.
    And say "I trust You, Lord, even
    though I may doubt."

R.I.O.T. ACT

Pray this prayer, *"I do believe; help me
overcome my unbelief!"* (Mark 9:24)

When you doubt the One Who has all the clout, remember to do your part, and God's Word will win out.

He Works with Me in Love

*And yet I see the way that He
Can work with me and do it all in love*

**"I HAVE LOVED YOU WITH AN EVERLASTING
LOVE; I HAVE DRAWN YOU WITH LOVING-
KINDNESS." (JEREMIAH 31:3)**

R.I.O.T.—RIGHTEOUS INVASION OF TRUTH

Ever feel unloved? Oh, I don't mean by mom or
dad, by friends or teachers, by pastors or preachers. I mean by God. Ever feel unloved by God? If
you ever do, here's a checklist of all the ways He's
shown His love for you:

- For you, He created water, air and food.
- For you, He made stars, sun and moon.
- For you, He gave parents, laughter and
  friends.
- For you, He gave giftings to serve His ends.
- For you, God gave His Son to die on the
  cross.
- For you, God gave healing and medicine to
  stop any loss.
- For you, God raised Jesus to give eternal life.
- For you, God created cats and dogs to put
  more spice in life.

- For you, God sent His Holy Spirit to comfort, counsel and help.
- For you, God waits. Just for you, to help.

R.I.O.T. ACT

Say this, *"For God so loves me, that He gave His only Son!"*

So don't be blue 'cause it's so true. No matter what you do, God loves you!

The Past is Gone!

*The past is gone, the future's long
And I need someone strong to help me through*

FORGET THE FORMER THINGS; DO NOT DWELL ON THE PAST. SEE, I [GOD] AM DOING A NEW THING! (ISAIAH 43:18-19)

R.I.O.T.—RIGHTEOUS INVASION OF TRUTH

Rick and Meagan were teenage lovers. As seniors in high school, they knew that they would marry as soon as they graduated. How excited they were! However, one problem got in their way. In the Fall of their senior year, Meagan got pregnant. Yes, they knew better. Yes, they loved God. Still, she was pregnant.

So what are you gonna do? Without so much as asking anyone, they decided an abortion was the easiest answer. No one knew. They quietly slipped across the state border that was only five miles away. Being eighteen, she could do what she liked. Rick had saved enough for the procedure. And except for a few weeks of physical discomfort, all seemed to go well.

But then it hit. Guilt. Meagan started feeling guilty and so did Rick. Every time they saw a baby, terrible, painful guilt would fill their hearts. They dreaded telling anyone even though they knew they would soon be married.

How can you bury the past and look ahead to a

42

bright future in such a mess? No sweat, what Meagan and Rick did was wrong, but it wasn't the end. They were sorry for their sin. And murder is a heavy one. But God could and would forgive them. Listen to His Promise, *"If we confess our sins, he is faithful and just to forgive us our sins and purify us from all unrighteousness."* (1 John 1:9)

If your past is forgiven, your future belongs to God. So ask His forgiveness. Move on.

R.I.O.T. ACT

Pray this, *"Lord Jesus, forgive my sin. I confess it and leave to You the rest!"*

Guilty? Then, repent. Confess. Give it up to God. Receive His forgiveness.

Just What Can the Power of God Do? Take the Vow!

I'm ready now to take the vow
And see just what the power of God can do
Well all right, okay, I guess it's up, up and away

BUT YOU WILL RECEIVE POWER WHEN THE HOLY SPIRIT COMES ON YOU; AND YOU WILL BE MY WITNESSES IN JERUSALEM, AND IN ALL JUDEA AND SAMARIA, AND TO THE ENDS OF THE EARTH. (ACTS 1:8)

R.I.O.T. — RIGHTEOUS INVASION OF TRUTH

The vacuum cleaner was not working. So, I worked on it. Cleaned the power sweep. Dumped all the dirt out of the bag. Replaced a belt in the power sweep that had snapped. And then, I turned on the cleaner and nothing happened. So, I began everything all over again. Checked everything including the motor. It all seemed fine. Then I happened to notice that the plug had pulled out of the socket. I couldn't get it working because it had no power! It's the same with you. You gotta be plugged into the power of Jesus Christ to have power to live this Christian life.

So check your life over. What keeps you out of

Christ's power flow? Unconfessed sin? Confess it. Anger and bitterness? Confess it. Hurt and pain? Surrender and confess it all to Jesus. He will remove every power block and energize you with His Holy Spirit to be a mighty warrior for Him. Then take a vow. Confess His Word. Speak your faith. Let the Holy Spirit watch over Jesus' Word and empower your life.

R.I.O.T. ACT

Stop "trying on your own" to trust Him and take the vow. *"It is written, I believed; therefore I have spoken.' With that same spirit of faith we also believe and therefore speak."* (2 Corinthians 4:13)

Turn on. Plug into Jesus. His Holy Spirit will empower you to say and to do.

Take That Step Now!

Take that step now
Keep goin', the left, the right, heel, toe, heel, toe
Well all right, okay, I guess I'll ride this horse away

AND WITHOUT FAITH IT IS IMPOSSIBLE TO PLEASE GOD, BECAUSE ANYONE WHO COMES TO HIM MUST BELIEVE THAT HE EXISTS AND THAT HE REWARDS THOSE WHO EARNESTLY SEEK HIM. (HEBREWS 11:6) WE LIVE BY FAITH, NOT BY SIGHT. (2 CORINTHIANS 5:7)

R.I.O.T.—RIGHTEOUS INVASION OF TRUTH

Dancin', we're dancin' through life,
Dance to the left, dance to the right,
We said we would follow wherever He leads,
He doesn't have to beg, doesn't have to plead.

Stepin', we're stepin' through life with Jesus Christ,
Step to the left, step to the right.
He promised to direct our steps each day,
'Cause He knows the direction, He is the Way.

Walkin', we're walkin' through life,
Walk to the left, walk to the right.
Jesus is the shining light on our walk,

So walking with Him we can walk
the talk.

Crawlin', sometimes we're just crawlin'
through life,
Barely crawlin' to the left or crawlin' to
the right.
Hey Christian, don't have to be
crawlin' around,
Jesus lifts you up, puts your feet
on solid ground.

Do it His way in getting from here to there,
In faith you walk not singly but in a pair,
So get ready to roll, get ready to go,
Always walk with Jesus, He will
carry your load.

R.I.O.T. ACT

Jesus said, *"Follow me."* (Luke 9:59)

Ready to stay in step with the Lord? Put your feet in His footprints, you'll never be bored!

Takin' a Giant Leap

Takin' a step, takin' a step of faith
Walkin' out on the promises God made
Takin' a giant leap in the air
Steppin' out on nothin' and findin' somethin' there

NOW FAITH IS BEING SURE OF WHAT WE HOPE FOR AND CERTAIN OF WHAT WE DO NOT SEE. (HEBREWS 11:1)

R.I.O.T.—RIGHTEOUS INVASION OF TRUTH

The boat rocked. The waves overwhelmed the small fishing craft. Holding on for their lives, the disciples look up and what do they see? A ghost? A spirit? A spook? In fear, they are scared out of their wits. "Don't fear, it is I," comes back the familiar voice of Jesus. Not quite believing his ears, Peter says, "If it's You, Lord, tell me to come." "Come on," Jesus invites. And you know what? Peter, an ordinary man, walked on water! If it wasn't for his faith he would have sunk. But he believed God's Word. And because he did, he might as well have been walking on solid ground!

Can you imagine trusting something you can't see? No way, you say. Oh really? Give me a break. You do it all the time every day. What? Trust the air you breathe? You can't see it but you trust it to keep you alive. What about someone you love? You've never seen their love but you trust it. We trust things we don't see all the time.

So here's the fact. We have faith in things unseen all the time. Question is—what or whom do you trust? Willing to step out of the boat with Peter? Or will you hang on to all your worldly ideas, fears and doubts? Jesus says, "Trust Me."

R.I.O.T. ACT

"Everything is possible for him who believes." (Mark 9:23)

Storms rage around you everyday. So, get out of the boat. Be a trusting lamb. Not an obstinate goat!

Doubt Can Wait

Tellin' the doubt to wait
I'm takin' a step of faith
Step of faith, step of faith

THE APOSTLES SAID TO THE LORD, "INCREASE OUR FAITH!" (LUKE 17:5)

R.I.O.T. — RIGHTEOUS INVASION OF TRUTH

How does faith grow? Much in the same way muscles grow. Want to get physically stronger? Then work out. As you work out and exercise your muscles, they will grow firmer and stronger.

Faith, like a muscle, also needs to be exercised. It has to be stretched to be strengthened. And there must be some resistance. Doing something that requires no faith will produce no faith. Like hanging out after school with the wrong crowd, talking their talk, getting worldly and loud. But start standing up for Jesus and you'll encounter a little resistance, along with God's blessing. Start sharing the Lord and praying for the sick and your faith, like a muscle, will grow strong and thick. Want to increase your faith? Then start takin' a step of faith, then another and another and another. Start working out.

So, the next time you pray and study the Bible, do what His Word says and trust Him to help you. Maybe His Word will direct you to pray or share with someone else. Ask Him for wisdom as you pray. When you do, you'll be blessed as He guides your day.

Faith doesn't begin lifting 200 pounds. It begins with ten, then grows in Him. So what keeps you from trusting God one step at a time? Start your faith workout! Get on with the climb!

R.I.O.T. ACT

"...Faith comes from hearing the message, and the message is heard through the word of Christ." (Romans 10:17)

Exercise your faith one step at a time. Jesus will be there to help you climb.

By Faith and Not By Sight

Living for the Lord, trusting in His care
Stepping out on nothing and finding something
there
Walking with the Lord, stepping in the light
living by our faith and not by sight

WE LIVE BY FAITH, NOT BY SIGHT. (2 CORINTHIANS 5:7)

R.I.O.T.—RIGHTEOUS INVASION OF TRUTH

Faith trusts Jesus. Not what we see, hear, feel or taste in the world. You see, our senses don't always tell us the truth. The world doesn't always tell us the truth. Our friends and parents don't always know or tell us all the truth. Teachers, preachers, leaders and other adults may mean well, but often they can't tell us what Jesus wants us to know.

So faith begins where our resources and the resources of others end. Faith starts where we on our own would stop. It goes beyond what we can do, think or accomplish. Faith sees what we can't see, hears what we can't hear, and does what we can't ordinarily do. It steps out into nothing and finds something there to do. Faith hears God's Word, and faithfully obeys, then talks it and walks it day by day.

So, what will it be? Have the world now and lose eternity? You don't have to wait on a relationship with Jesus. That can happen now. Now faith has substance. Walk with Jesus now.

R.I.O.T. ACT

"Now faith is being sure of what we hope for and certain of what we do not see." (Hebrews 11:1)

Tempted now? Trust, don't go bust. Jesus is the only One you can trust.

When the Devil Comes to Your Door

*The devil came to my house, knocked on my door
I said, oh my, I know that I have heard
this voice before*

JESUS, FULL OF THE HOLY SPIRIT, RETURNED FROM THE JORDAN AND WAS LED BY THE SPIRIT IN THE DESERT, WHERE FOR FORTY DAYS HE WAS TEMPTED BY THE DEVIL. (LUKE 4:1-2)

R.I.O.T.—RIGHTEOUS INVASION OF TRUTH

Yes, that's right. The devil does show up at your door. Say what? Say, that's reality. As long as you and I are alive, the devil will tempt, lie, and try to make us serve him. Why? He wants to rob glory from God. He wants to render you powerless. He may have lost you for eternity, but right now he's doing damage control. If he can keep Christians like you and me powerless, then we won't win others to Jesus or make trouble for him.

Now just a couple pointers for when the devil shows up!

- He's been around a lot longer than you...and often knows your weaknesses better than you. So don't argue or debate with Satan. Jesus didn't, He simply said, "It is written."

In other words, "Don't care what you say devil, 'cause God says..." then speak the Word of God!

- The devil's always trying the same old tricks and treats. He appeals to your lusts, your senses, your self-desires. So look out for who Satan may be sending your way.

- Finally, the devil would like to give you what you want so he can use it for himself. So here's the temptation, ever thought this thought? *If I just had that [whatever it is you want, not what you need], then I could [do whatever I want]?* So look out for those selfish desires and wants.

R.I.O.T. ACT

"Submit yourselves, then, to God. Resist the devil, and he will flee from you." (James 4:7)

Devil, don't come to my door. Ain't nobody home to meet you no more.

The Devil Wants To Make You a Star

*He said you're quite a talent, the makings of a star
And with a little help from me, you really can go far*

...AND YOU WILL BE LIKE GOD, KNOWING GOOD AND EVIL [THE SERPENT TEMPTED EVE]. (GENESIS 3:5)

R.I.O.T.—RIGHTEOUS INVASION OF TRUTH

Cathy dreamed of being a cheerleader. She could picture herself in front of hundreds of fans leading them in great cheers for the team. They would all look at her, admire, and follow her. She would be in the yearbook and be noticed by all the guys—especially Tom. What a hunk! If she could just make the squad, all her dreams would come true.

Wrong. Lie. Hear the deception? We are often tempted by our desires to get glory for ourselves instead of God. "I" always gets in the way of our relationship with God. The devil goes for our egos. He tempts us by suggesting he can make us stars. Or to become more popular, more athletic, more beautiful, more handsome, more intelligent than those around us. So, *who ya gonna shine for?* Gonna let the devil make you a star? If you do you'll burn out—you won't go very far. Oh you may make it big and all may seem well. But one day he'll take you right to hell!

Truth is, in Jesus Christ you are becoming a shining star through the power of His Light. His Light doesn't burn out. So shine for His glory, not yours. Light the darkness with His Light, not your own. Philippians 2:14-16 reads, *"Do everything without complaining or arguing, so that you may become blameless and pure, children of God without fault in a crooked and depraved generation, in which you shine like stars in the universe as you hold out the word of life...."* The word of life is Jesus. Shine for Him!

R.I.O.T. ACT

"I am the light of the world. Whoever follows me will never walk in darkness, but will have the light of life." (John 8:12)

Devil, take the next flight 'cause Jesus, not you, is my light!

Who Gets the Glory?

I'll tell you what I've told the rest, the rules remain the same
Don't glorify, support or even mention Jesus' name

THAT AT THE NAME OF JESUS EVERY KNEE SHOULD BOW, IN HEAVEN AND ON EARTH AND UNDER THE EARTH, AND EVERY TONGUE CONFESS THAT JESUS CHRIST IS LORD, TO THE GLORY OF GOD THE FATHER. (PHILIPPIANS 2:10-11)

R.I.O.T.—RIGHTEOUS INVASION OF TRUTH

John was valedictorian of his class at the largest public high school in the region. For four years he had dreamed of this. He had worked hard for the opportunity to be on the top, to be recognized as the smartest and the best in his class of 800 seniors. The night of commencement had arrived. He would not only be recognized as valedictorian and receive the special scholarship presentation, he would also have the privilege of giving the valedictorian's speech. Over 2,000 people would be there listening to him. What an honor. What glory!

However, there was one catch. The principal knew that John was a committed Christian. So, the principal had asked John not to mention his faith in his speech out of respect for those who might be of a different religion. John wrestled for days over his speech. It just wasn't coming together. He wrestled with these thoughts. *It's not so hard to not mention Jesus. After all, this is my night of recognition, not His. I worked for this and earned this.* They kept him up at night and played havoc with his sleep. But in the end, John did the right thing. He thanked the Lord in public for giving him his gifts.

What would you do?

R.I.O.T. ACT

"To him who sits on the throne and to the Lamb be praise and honor and glory and power, for ever and ever!" (Revelation 5:13)

The choice is about the Bible's story. Do I or does He receive the glory?

YOU Can Save Somebody

Now you can do something that's positive, but just don't misbehave
Like use your notoriety and get somebody saved

BUT YOU WILL RECEIVE POWER WHEN THE HOLY SPIRIT COMES ON YOU; AND YOU WILL BE MY WITNESSES.... (ACTS 1:8)

R. I. O. T. — RIGHTEOUS INVASION OF TRUTH

Now here's a subtle temptation—*to do something FOR Jesus instead of WITH Jesus*. Believe it or not, Jesus doesn't need your help, your suggestions or your advice. In fact, He doesn't need you. True, He loves you. But He doesn't need you.

One of the greatest temptations the devil has is to get us to draw back from sharing our faith. "Do you want to be embarrassed or make a fool out of yourself? What about So-and-so and don't you know, your friends will laugh..." Oh devil, blow!

I'm tempted to use my position and status for my own fame. Just like you, whenever I do something and others look at me, the devil's right there to give me the glory. What a temptation. What a lie! Remember the text from Acts 1? Jesus says "My witnesses." We belong to Him. We witness for Him, not for ourselves. So this message is simple.

God gave my fame to proclaim His name. If I got worldly, and went sour on the deal, Satan would move in to kill and steal. Use your reputation to get others saved, stay solid in Jesus every day.

R.I.O.T. ACT

"So the word of God spread. The number of disciples in Jerusalem increased rapidly, and a large number of priests became obedient to the faith." *(Acts 6:7)*

Don't buy the lie. Testify!

Where You Gonna Leave Your Faith?

And don't you be so vocal about the truth you know
The Bible's bad for business, leave your
faith at home

TAKE THE HELMET OF SALVATION AND THE SWORD OF THE SPIRIT, WHICH IS THE WORD OF GOD. (EPHESIANS 6:17)

R.I.O.T.—RIGHTEOUS INVASION OF TRUTH

Who ya gonna talk about when the people
    want to know,
      how you get your inspiration,
        and how you get up and go?

Who ya gonna speak about when fame comes
    knockin' at your door,
      and offers fans and wealth,
        with all life's pleasures laid up in store?

Who ya gonna seek to please when agents
    offer you the moon,
      and all you have to do is compromise,
        and sing the devil's tune?

Who ya gonna worship when they shoot your
    celebrity shot,
      and people want your photos and autograph
        a lot?

Who ya gonna turn to when everything goes
    your way,

and people want to do your bidding by
telling you what to say?

Who ya gonna turn to when all the lights go off,
and in the emptiness of your room,
there's no one left to be bought?

Who ya gonna turn to before the fame and
lights,
and you have to make decisions,
and to know what's wrong or right?

The only one to start with is the one who will
be there at the end,
My friend it ain't the devil,
Only Jesus is your friend.

R.I.O.T. ACT

Start and end with Jesus and you will never
have to wonder how, when, where, or why! *"And
surely I* [Jesus] *am with you always, to the very
end of the age." (Matthew 28:20)*

**In the end, only Jesus will be your
friend. He's the One Who gives you
gifts and puts you here or there. It's
the fallen cherub Lucifer who
wants to take you unaware.**

Can We Live the Way We Want?

I'll give you wealth and fame, far as the eye can see
Live the way you want, but your career
belongs to me

DO YOU NOT KNOW THAT YOUR BODY IS A TEMPLE OF THE HOLY SPIRIT, WHO IS IN YOU, WHOM YOU HAVE RECEIVED FROM GOD? YOU ARE NOT YOUR OWN; YOU WERE BOUGHT AT A PRICE. THEREFORE HONOR GOD WITH YOUR BODY. (1 CORINTHIANS 6:19-20)

R.I.O.T.—RIGHTEOUS INVASION OF TRUTH

He really wanted to follow Jesus. And, he was a great guy. In fact, if you had personally known him, you would have admired him. He loved God and obeyed all the commandments. In fact, he never seemed to do anything wrong. He was a good guy. Problem was, good ain't good enough.

You see, even good guys are still holding on to something—even if it's only their goodness. This guy I'm talking about couldn't let go of his money. He wanted to follow Jesus but his money got in the way. He did the right things, mind you, but not every day.

So Jesus says to this rich guy, *One thing you lack... Go, sell everything you have and give to the poor, and you will have treasure in heaven. Then come, follow me. (Mark 10:21)*

That sounded crazy to this rich guy. So he turned away all down and saddened and slowly walked away. So Jesus said, "Hey, get this handle? It's harder for the rich to get saved than to thread a needle with a camel." The problem with wealth and careers is that we try to use them as our source. But what Jesus provides will never fade away. What are you holding onto? Who is your source?

R.I.O.T. ACT

"For where your treasure is, there your heart will be also." (Matthew 6:21)

That which I possess, possesses me. Jesus is all I ever need.

More Than a Necklace or an Earring

Then he smiled a crooked smile and winked
an evil eye
And said "Well, what do you think, my man?" and
this was my reply
I have been bought with a price when Jesus hung
on a tree

FOR THE MESSAGE OF THE CROSS IS FOOLISHNESS TO THOSE WHO ARE PERISHING, BUT TO US WHO ARE BEING SAVED IT IS THE POWER OF GOD.... (1 CORINTHIANS 1:18)

R.I.O.T.—RIGHTEOUS INVASION OF TRUTH

It's more than jewelry that you wear around your neck or in your ear. It's more than gold or silver, pewter or steel. It's more than a symbol on a steeple or an altar in a church. It's more than a decoration in homes or cars. It's more than an object of art or conversation. In fact, it's both beautiful and ugly: It's the cross. Jesus Christ paid the price for our salvation on this agonizing altar.

We cheapen the cross and God's grace when we forget the price He paid for our sins. Listen to

Jesus' agony described in Psalm 22:14-17:

I am poured out like water, and all my bones are out of joint. My heart has turned to wax; it has melted away within me. My strength is dried up like a potsherd, and my tongue sticks to the roof of my mouth; you lay me in the dust of death. Dogs have surrounded me; a band of evil men has encircled me, they have pierced my hands and my feet. I can count all my bones; people stare and gloat over me.

What a price He paid for our salvation. Think about it. The next time you see Jesus' cross on the altar or on top of a steeple, praise the Lord for His suffering that redeemed every people.

R.I.O.T. ACT

"He himself bore our sins in his body on the tree, so that we might die to sins and live for righteousness; by his wounds you have been healed." (1 Peter 2:24)

Show the devil who's the boss—don't just wear it, live the cross!

Bought With a Price

*Then he smiled a crooked smile and winked an evil eye
And said "Well, what do you think, my man?" and this
was my reply
I have been bought with a price when Jesus hung on a tree*

**FOR THE MESSAGE OF THE CROSS IS FOOLISHNESS
TO THOSE WHO ARE PERISHING, BUT TO US WHO
ARE BEING SAVED IT IS THE POWER OF GOD....
YOU ARE NOT YOUR OWN; YOU WERE BOUGHT
AT A PRICE. THEREFORE HONOR GOD WITH
YOUR BODY. (1 CORINTHIANS 1:18; 6:19,20)**

R.I.O.T.—RIGHTEOUS INVASION OF TRUTH

How much would you pay for...
> a house?
> > a car?
> > > a CD player?
> > > > a computer?
> > > > > a new outfit?
> > > > > > a boat?

How much would you pay for...
> love?
> > truth?
> > > integrity?
> > > > moral purity?
> > > > > character?

How much would you pay for...
> freedom?
> > healing?
> > > deliverance?
> > > > joy?
> > > > > salvation?

Some say everything has a price,
>But not everything is for sale,
>>And some things just can't be bought
>>>'cause the price is too high.

Take salvation—being saved from sin and saved
for eternal life.
>How much does it cost?
>>Who pays the price?
>>>Who gets the benefit?

Cost? The cross.
>Who paid? Only one could and He did
>—Jesus.
>>Who benefits? All who trust Jesus as
>>Lord and Savior.

That says it.
>That settles it.
>>Will you accept it?

R.I.O.T. ACT

The wages of sin is death. Either yours or some-body else's. Only one man can die for you. His name is Jesus. For Him, the cost was high. To you, it's free. Accept it! *"You are not your own; you were bought at a price." (1 Corinthians 6:19,20)*

The cross of Jesus destroys the work of the evil one. Believe it! Accept it! It is done!

My Life Is not My Own

My life is not my own, I'll never follow your lead

SET YOUR MINDS ON THINGS ABOVE, NOT ON EARTHLY THINGS. FOR YOU DIED, AND YOUR LIFE IS NOW HIDDEN WITH CHRIST IN GOD. (COLOSSIANS 3:2-3)

R.I.O.T.—RIGHTEOUS INVASION OF TRUTH

To what or whom do you belong? For some, belonging to a certain school is important. Others belong to churches, or clubs, or sports teams or certain social groups. Other types of belongings include family, race and religion. To what or whom do you belong?

If my life is not my own, then who do I belong to? I could belong to my parents, but they don't own me. God has entrusted me to their care. I could belong to my boss, but he doesn't own me. I could belong to my boyfriend or girlfriend, but they don't own me. So who do I belong to? I belong to Jesus. He is my Creator and my owner too.

So am I a slave? Sort of, better to say "servant." Jesus says, *"...Whoever wants to become great among you must be your servant."* (Matthew 20:26) Servants belong to their master. But Jesus said we are more than servants. In John 15:14 He said we are His friends, that is, if we obey His Word. Friends spend time with one another and share their thoughts.

So stop trying to work your way to the top. Stop struggling, scratching, biting, and pushing so hard to be king of the mountain. That's what the devil wants you to do. The busier he can keep you, the less time you have to serve Jesus.

R.I.O.T. ACT

"You are my friends if you do what I command. I no longer call you servants, because a servant does not know his master's business. Instead, I have called you friends, for everything that I learned from my Father I have made known to you." (John 15:14-15)

It takes nerve to serve!

Oh, Be Careful Eyes What You See!

*You build up all the pleasure of sin in people's eyes
But never tell the consequences of the compromise
You used to have my number, but this time you will
fail*

FOR EVERYTHING IN THE WORLD—THE CRAVINGS OF SINFUL MAN, THE LUST OF HIS EYES AND THE BOASTING OF WHAT HE HAS AND DOES—COMES NOT FROM THE FATHER BUT FROM THE WORLD. (1 JOHN 2:16)

R.I.O.T.—RIGHTEOUS INVASION OF TRUTH

A children's song goes something like this...
> Oh be careful little eyes what you see,
> For the Father up above is looking down
> in love,
> So be careful little eyes what you see.

This is good advice! Satan's goal is to build up the pleasure of sin in people's eyes so that they will be tempted to act on it. Sin appeals to our lusts and other sinful desires that seek only what can give us the most pleasure and fun just for the moment. This is the mind of the world.

The Bible tells us to avoid loving the world. *"Do not love the world or anything in the world....*

The world and its desires pass away, but the man who does the will of God lives forever." (1 John 2:15,17) So think about what you allow your eyes to look upon or your ears to hear. Your mind and spirit are just like a piece of film. Whatever you expose them to is going to develop. Expose yourself to rot and glop and it will develop in bad news thinking patterns and vain imaginations.

The first step toward sin is often a small one. Sow a thought, reap an action. Sow an action, reap a habit. Sow a bad habit—and you've got a problem that could have been avoided by simply changing the channel, choosing not to see that movie, or by simply, walking away.

R.I.O.T. ACT

"Avoid every kind of evil."
(1 Thessalonians 5:22)

What's all the fuss? Just say "No!" to lust!

Sowing and Reaping

You build up all the pleasure of sin in people's eyes
But never tell the consequences of the compromise
You used to have my number, but this time you will
fail

DO NOT BE DECEIVED: GOD CANNOT BE MOCKED. A MAN REAPS WHAT HE SOWS. (GALATIANS 6:7)

R.I.O.T.—RIGHTEOUS INVASION OF TRUTH

Chris thought he could get away with his favorite passion. He loved oreo cookie blizzards from Dairy Queen. At first, nobody could tell that he ate one every day using his lunch money. But after a few weeks passed, everyone began to notice that Chris was gaining weight. Soon, he had gained over fifteen pounds. It seemed so harmless, eating just one a day. But over a period of time, Chris really grew to be amazingly fat. So fat, he needed to buy new clothes and a new hat.

Sowing and reaping. What we sow now, we reap later. Harvest doesn't happen right away, but eventually it comes. If we sow to oreo cookie blizzards, we won't notice a problem the first few days. But don't be deceived. After time passes, the blizzards will give a harvest of pounds. And that's not just true with blizzards! You can even do it with tuna and oatmeal!

If we sow hate, the harvest will be others

hating us. If we sow love, we'll harvest love. If we sow immoral, impure behavior, we grieve the Holy Spirit and find ourselves in a world of hurt. If we sow mercy, we obtain a harvest of forgiveness.

So, what kind of consequences are you sowing into your life? Are you sowing good seed? Or are you sowing strife? Are you sowing for a harvest of righteousness? Or are you poisoning your garden with pettiness?

R.I.O.T. ACT

Sow good seed and God will meet your every need. *(Mark 4:20)*

Want truth and holiness in your life? Sow God's Word—live life right!

Get Behind Me, Satan

So get thee behind me, Satan, I'm not for sale.

JESUS TURNED AND SAID TO PETER, "GET BEHIND ME, SATAN! YOU ARE A STUMBLING BLOCK TO ME; YOU DO NOT HAVE IN MIND THE THINGS OF GOD, BUT THE THINGS OF MEN. (MATTHEW 16:23)

R.I.O.T.—RIGHTEOUS INVASION OF TRUTH

Kyle and Bryce were best friends. They went everywhere and did everything together. Tonight was the big party at Noel's house. Both went together and walked in on a wild gig that had booze flowing everywhere. Some were also smoking pot and everyone seemed either drunk or stoned.

Kyle wanted to leave. But Bryce pressed him to stay. "Lighten up, man, you can enjoy the party without feeling guilty. Have a drink. Have a little fun in your life," Bryce urged. Kyle knew they didn't need to be there but Bryce was his best friend. He couldn't just dump him there and leave. Funny, isn't it? Sometimes, it's your best friends who tempt you to do the worst things. Somehow, the devil finds a way to work through them.

Same thing happened to Jesus. On the road to

Caesarea Philippi, Jesus is talking with His disciples about who He is. Then one of his most faithful friends, Peter, confesses that Jesus is God's Son. But soon after that, this same friend tried to get Jesus to avoid the suffering and death that would destroy Satan's work on the cross. In other words, best friend, Peter, tried to get Jesus to do just the opposite of God's will. When Jesus responded, He did so quickly and harshly, "Get behind me, Satan!" So should you when any of your so called friends try to get you to take a dive.

R.I.O.T. ACT

"Do not be misled: *'Bad company corrupts good character.'*" *(1 Corinthians 15:33)*

Where Jesus leads, you must go. If your friends don't want to— tell them to blow!

Supernatural Testimony

*93 million miles from the blistering surface of the
sun hangs planet earth
A rotating sphere perfectly suspended in the center
of the universe
The ultimate creation from an infinite mind
A supernatural testimony, an irrefutable sign.*

**THIS IS WHAT GOD THE LORD SAYS—HE
WHO CREATED THE HEAVENS AND
STRETCHED THEM OUT, WHO SPREAD OUT
THE EARTH AND ALL THAT COMES OUT OF
IT, WHO GIVES BREATH TO ITS PEOPLE,
AND LIFE TO THOSE WHO WALK ON IT.
(ISAIAH 42:5)**

R.I.O.T.—RIGHTEOUS INVASION OF TRUTH

Imagine you had never seen a computer
before. Computers are wonderfully complex and
capable of doing thousands of computations per
second. You walk into a store and see your first
computer. When the sales representative intro-
duces herself you ask her, "Now who makes this
computer?" Then she glibly responds, "No one, it
just happened." Right. A computer so intricately
engineered, had to have a creative engineer. Without a creator, creations don't exist.

Yet, that's what some sophisticated scientists

would have you to believe when you gaze out upon the universe. Bang! Something happened. Then it evolved. Give me "the" holy break! The odds of this happening are the same as if you were to smash your wrist-watch in a paper bag, shake it up, and pour it out reassembled and working intact. Not!

Truth is, *"In the beginning, God created the heavens and the earth."* (Genesis 1:1) Doesn't take Einstein or Carl Sagan to figure that one out, man. Look all around you at all of life. Only God could have engineered a universe so awesome and life so amazing! Get the picture? God created.

R.I.O.T. ACT

"In the beginning was the Word...Through him [Jesus] all things were made; without him nothing was made that has been made." (John 1:1,3)

We weren't accidentally fated. Get real and tell others, we're created!

The Invisible Things

The size, position and angle of the earth is a scientific phenomenon to see
A few degrees closer to the sun we'd disintegrate, a few degrees further we'd freeze
The axis of the earth is tilted at a perfect 23 degree angle and it's no mistake that it is
This allows equal global distribution to the rays of the sun making it possible
for the food chain to exist
Or take for example the combination of nitrogen and oxygen in the atmosphere we breathe everyday
It just happens to be the exact mix that life needs to prosper, it doesn't happen on any other planet that way
You see, the Bible says the invisible things of God are clearly seen through His creation,
to believe this is not hard

FOR SINCE THE CREATION OF THE WORLD GOD'S INVISIBLE QUALITIES—HIS ETERNAL POWER AND DIVINE NATURE—HAVE BEEN CLEARLY SEEN, BEING UNDERSTOOD FROM WHAT HAS BEEN MADE, SO THAT MEN ARE WITHOUT EXCUSE. (ROMANS 1:20)

R.I.O.T.—RIGHTEOUS INVASION OF TRUTH

Take a flower, what do you see?
>   Beauty. That's plain to you and me.
Take a sunset, what do you see?
>   Grandeur. This too is plain to see.
Now take a baby cuddled in your arms. What do you see?
>   Gentleness. That's plain enough.

But take the creation of the world and some
folks get in a huff. Why?
They're all hung up on this monkey stuff.
Could the sun, moon and stars, and our little
planet have exploded out of nothing—
with no one to plan it? Monkey stuff says,
"Yeah, that's cool!"
But as for me and my house, I ain't no
fool!

God's signature is everywhere,
Sun, stars and moon,
Creatures everywhere—including
BABOONS,
Don't have to have been there at the signing,
to know what God's done,
He's always been there—eternally
designing!

R.I.O.T. ACT

Redeemer, Creator, our Maker is He. Confess
God as all, all is He! *"It is he who made us, and we
are his."* (Psalm 100:3)

Satan, the snake, is a counterfeit
or fake. Ain't no degree or white
professor smock heavy enough to
make me believe that "scientific"
glop!

There's A Designer

If there's a design, there's a designer; if there's a plan, there's a planner, and if there's a miracle, there is a God.

IN HIM WE WERE ALSO CHOSEN, HAVING BEEN PREDESTINED ACCORDING TO THE PLAN OF HIM WHO WORKS OUT EVERYTHING IN CONFORMITY WITH THE PURPOSE OF HIS WILL. (EPHESIANS 1:11)

R.I.O.T.—RIGHTEOUS INVASION OF TRUTH

You are a miracle. Look at yourself in a mirror. No accident created you. There was someone who planned you down to the last fingernail and eyelash. One knew your end before your beginning. One designed your blood cells and fine tuned your nerve cells. One developed your organs, bones and flesh. Listen to what David thought about this:

For you created my inmost being;
   you knit me together in my mother's womb.
I praise you because I am fearfully and
   wonderfully made;
   your works are wonderful, I know that full
   well.
My frame was not hidden from you when I was
   made in the secret place.
   When I was woven together in the depths of
   the earth,
   your eyes saw my unformed body.

*All the days ordained for me were written in
your book
before one of them came to be. (Psalm
139:13-16)*

You may have been told by your parents that
you were an accident, unplanned. But know this,
before He ever creates, God starts with a design,
purpose, and plan. You were created with purpose, to fulfill His plan.

R.I.O.T. ACT

So, look in the mirror and say, God made me.
He has a plan in Jesus just for me. You are a creative act. *"And I pray that you, being rooted and
established in love, may have power, together with
all the saints, to grasp how wide and long and
high and deep is the love of Christ, and to know
this love that surpasses knowledge—that you may
be filled to the measure of all the fullness of God."*
(Ephesians 3:17-19)

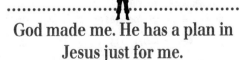

God made me. He has a plan in Jesus just for me.

There is a God

There is a hope
There is a light
There is an answer to all answers
There is a flame that burns in the night
And I know, I know there is a God.

IN HIM WAS LIFE, AND THAT LIFE WAS THE LIGHT OF MEN. THE LIGHT SHINES IN THE DARKNESS, BUT THE DARKNESS HAS NOT UNDERSTOOD IT. (JOHN 1:4,5)

R.I.O.T.—RIGHTEOUS INVASION OF TRUTH

In the middle of the darkest night, go into a room. Then get a candle, match or flashlight. With every curtain drawn, every blind closed, make certain that it's pitch black. Now, light the candle. Strike the match. Then, turn on the flashlight. Try as it will, the darkness can't overcome it. One small light can curse the darkness. One small light can bring sight to the blind. One small light can reveal whatever is hidden.

Jesus said, *"I am the light of the world. Whoever follows me will never walk in darkness, but will have the light of life."(John 8:12)* No matter how deep and dark your night, Jesus can light it. He can make things bright!

Have a dark sin that blots your life? Bring it to Jesus. He forgives. He's the light. He will over-come the darkness and make it fade away. Have a friend living in darkness? Don't delay. Bring him or her to Jesus. He's the light. He forgives and saves. He will turn things around and make them right.

R.I.O.T. ACT

"For God, who said, 'Let light shine out of darkness,' made his light shine in our hearts to give us the light of the knowledge of the glory of God in the face of Christ." (2 Corinthians 4:6)

Curse the night. Come to Jesus—He's the light!

Declare God's Glory

*The Scripture says the heavens declare the glory of God
and the skies proclaim the work of His hands*

THE HEAVENS DECLARE THE GLORY OF GOD; THE SKIES PROCLAIM THE WORK OF HIS HANDS. (PSALM 19:1)

R.I.O.T.—RIGHTEOUS INVASION OF TRUTH

"Let's party late Saturday night and then we'll sleep in on Sunday morning," came the invitation from Kia's best friend, Amber. Problem. Kia is a strong Christian. Amber knew that, but she was putting Kia's faith to the test. Kia was a leader in her youth group. Every Sunday morning she was a greeter at the door and welcomed anyone new to the group. Sure, Kia could and did miss on occasion. But to plan to miss and party instead...that didn't fit with her convictions or witness for Jesus.

It's one thing to declare God's glory at a beautiful sunset or gazing up at a stunning, starlit night. It's not hard to declare God's glory standing in the midst of a group of Christians at church when everyone agrees with what you're saying. But, it's something else to declare God's glory to a friend who may not know Jesus or understand your values and beliefs. Or to declare God's glory in a biology class when the teacher claims there is no God and that we all evolved from a primordial bog. Or to declare God's glory at a wild party when the host offers you a beer.

Kia turned down Amber's party invitation. So how about you? Will you declare God's glory no matter where you are at or what your circumstances are? Will you be bold, strong and mighty for God? Are you willing to declare His glory no matter what?

R.I.O.T. ACT

"I am not ashamed of the gospel, because it is the power of God for the salvation of everyone who believes...." (Romans 1:16)

No matter what the situation or the story, make a decision now to declare God's glory!

Truth Surrounds Us

If we allow our minds to drink in all the truth that just surrounds us,
creation itself will help us understand
Did you know the moon controls the tides, it's the maid that cleans the oceans,
even the waves don't crash the shores in vain
The tides drag impurities into the depths of the sea, it's nature's constant recycling chain
It simply boggles the mind to think that the stars will rotate with such exact precision that
it s true
That the atomic clock with an error factor of less than three seconds per millennium is set by the
way they move

FOR SINCE THE CREATION OF THE WORLD GOD'S INVISIBLE QUALITIES—HIS ETERNAL POWER AND DIVINE NATURE—HAVE BEEN CLEARLY SEEN... (ROMANS 1:20)

R.I.O.T.—RIGHTEOUS INVASION OF TRUTH

His intense stare and fiery eyes riveted on every listener. The place was Athens, Greece. The time was around 45 A.D. The man was Paul. Imagine you were there. Listen to his words:

Men of Athens! I see that in every way you are very religious. For as I walked around and looked carefully at your objects of worship, I even found an altar with this inscription: TO AN UNKNOWN GOD. Now what you worship as something unknown I am going to proclaim to you. The God who made the world and everything in it is the Lord of heaven and earth and does not live in temples built by hands." (Acts 17:22b-24)

The apostle then went on to declare that this same God—Creator of the universe—would resurrect all humanity at the end of time and judge the world with justice. These Greeks needed to know this "unknown God," and Paul introduced them to Him. They could see His creation, but could only guess at Who He was.

Do you know this personal, Creator God that Paul spoke of long ago? If you don't, pray this, "God, reveal Yourself to me in Your Son Jesus Christ." Then, consider the sun, the Big Dipper, or a moonlit night. Who put them there? Did they really just sort of scatter around then accidentally roll into place?

R.I.O.T. ACT

"And if you look for it as for silver and search for it as for hidden treasure, then you will understand the fear of the Lord and find the knowledge of God." (Proverbs 2:4-5)

Look in the Book—search out
His ways. Acknowledge Him,
trust in Him—He'll help you all
your days.

What the Fool Says

*Though they silently orbit, the sun, the moon, the
stars are like celestial evangelists above
Who circle the earth every 24 hours shouting in
every language that there is a God
Atheism is the wedge under the foundation of our
faith trying to topple our
relationship with Christ
Then the fool said in his heart, there is no God, he
rejects the truth God painted on the canvas
of the night*

**THE FOOL SAYS IN HIS HEART, "THERE IS
NO GOD." THEY ARE CORRUPT, THEIR
DEEDS ARE VILE; THERE IS NO ONE WHO
DOES GOOD. (PSALM 14:1)**

R.I.O.T.—RIGHTEOUS INVASION OF TRUTH

So what's a fool? Surprisingly enough, fools
may have lots of education and sophisticated
degrees. They can come in all shapes and sizes, all
ethnic and religious backgrounds. Some fools are
rich. Others are poor. Some fools are old—others
twenty-four. Only one thing makes you a fool, and
it has nothing to do with dumb or smart. A fool has
no place for God in his heart.

A fool rejects the truth. A fool sees creation and
denies the Creator. A fool believes he can save
himself. He doesn't believe in right or wrong. He
comes right out and says there is no God. Fools

are atheists whether they admit it or not. They may say they believe, but really, not. They don't pray. They don't believe. They don't trust Jesus. Fools think they are in control. But fools are so foolish, they don't really know.

So don't be a fool. Open your eyes. Don't let the fool's wisdom delude you with lies.

R.I.O.T. ACT

"A wise man [or woman] fears the Lord and shuns evil, but a fool is hotheaded and reckless." (Proverbs 14:16)

A fool like a mule stubbornly goes his own way. Don't be a fool, follow Jesus today.

Atheism Has Never...

Atheism has never created an artistic masterpiece,
never healed a fatal disease or carried a fear
Atheism has never still given answers to our
existence,
peace to a troubled mind or even dried a tear

PRAISE THE LORD, O MY SOUL, AND FORGET NOT ALL HIS BENEFITS—WHO FORGIVES ALL YOUR SINS AND HEALS ALL YOUR DISEASES, WHO REDEEMS YOUR LIFE FROM THE PIT AND CROWNS YOU WITH LOVE AND COMPASSION, WHO SATISFIES YOUR DESIRES WITH GOOD THINGS SO THAT YOUR YOUTH IS RENEWED LIKE THE EAGLE'S. (PSALM 103:2-5)

R.I.O.T.—RIGHTEOUS INVASION OF TRUTH

Atheist,

> Who can create a sunset, thunderstorm or sunrise?
>
> Who can make a fish swim or a bird that flies?
>
> Who can heal a cough, cold or the flu?
>
> If you can't do this, then who?

Atheist,

> Can you lift a person from despair, give them a reason to care?
>
> Can you convince a suicide there's a reason to live or a miser there's a reason to give?

92

Can you love forever and never divorce,
    give a good reason to stay to those on
    course?
Can you persuade the skeptic to have
    hope, and the depressed not to mope?
Atheist,
    You've got a problem, it's easy to see—you
    can't convince yourself, much less
    others or me.

Only God can give hope and a reason to live.
Only God creates goodness and lives to give.
Without God, the atheist blunders. With God he
can seek God's wonders.

R.I.O.T. ACT

"...And whoever comes to me I will never drive away." (John 6:37)

Atheist, don't run and hide, get on God's side.

It's God Who...

*For it's God Who created heaven and earth and
flung the stars in space and breathed
a handful of dirt and it became a man
It's God who sits on the circle of the earth and
measures the mountain in a scale,
and holds the seven seas in the palm of His hand*

**SO GOD CREATED MAN IN HIS OWN IMAGE,
IN THE IMAGE OF GOD HE CREATED HIM;
MALE AND FEMALE HE CREATED THEM.
(GENESIS 1:27)**

R.I.O.T.—RIGHTEOUS INVASION OF TRUTH

Fish and birds, streams and rivers, trees and flowers were not enough. God wasn't finished yet. Stars and moon, planets and solar systems, black holes and galaxies, were not enough. Volcanoes, mountains, valleys and grand canyons, and still, God wasn't finished yet.

God created sun, moon and stars.
That's good, He said.
Created earth and oceans.
That's good too, He said.
Created trees, flowers and grass.
That's good, He said.
Created birds and fish.
That's good too, He said.
Created animals and all living creatures.
That's good, He said.

Then God created male and female.
    And it was very, very good.
Then He was finished. Because after all,
    He made it for them to rule over all.

God isn't finished with you yet. His creative power is at work in you transforming you into the likeness of Jesus to represent Him on earth. Created in His image! Created in God's image! We are becoming more a reflection of His glory every day. *"And we, who with unveiled faces all reflect the Lord's glory, are being transformed into his likeness with ever-increasing glory, which comes from the Lord, who is the Spirit." (2 Corinthians 3:18)*

R.I.O.T. ACT

Thank God for specially creating you today! *"Therefore, if anyone is in Christ, he is a new creation...." (2 Corinthians 5:17)*

Created in His image. Broken by sin. Recreated by His Spirit through Jesus from within!

God Sent His Only Son

*It's God who sent His only begotten Son to the cross
of Calvary to save our souls
from hell and the grave*

**FOR GOD SO LOVED THE WORLD, THAT HE
GAVE HIS ONLY BEGOTTEN SON, THAT
WHOSOEVER BELIEVETH IN HIM SHOULD
NOT PERISH, BUT HAVE EVERLASTING LIFE.
(JOHN 3:16 KJV)**

R.I.O.T.—RIGHTEOUS INVASION OF TRUTH

Once there were ninety-nine sheep already in the fold, but the shepherd went out into the cold. He searched and he looked until He found, just the one, not the many, it was you, that He found. (Luke 15) For whom did Jesus die? For murderers and crooks, for liars and thieves, for rich and for poor, for you and for me.

If something very valuable to you was lost, how much effort would you expend to find it? Lots? Think of it this way. Your house is burning. There's time to find and save only one thing in it. What would you dart into the house to save?

Think of it another way. A person is in that burning house. And things are so bad that if you run in to save him, you could push him out of the

96

window. But you would die in the process. Would you do it?

Finally, think of Jesus' love in this way. A hated enemy is in the house. He has killed and hurt others. He doesn't deserve to live. And, if you save him, he'd probably kill you in return. Would you go in to save him? All of this is comparable to what Jesus did for you. You were lost, you were burning and you fought against the Lord. But Jesus got you out of the house, then died for you inside.

R.I.O.T. ACT

Thank Jesus and tell someone else about His blood today! *"He* [Jesus] *was delivered over to death for our sins and was raised to life for our justification." (Romans 4:25)*

- -

We were enemies. Lost and condemned. Jesus came and died for us and washed us free from sin.

- -

God Is Worthy of All Praise

It's God who creates, God who delivers, God who heals and God who is worthy of a thunderous ovation of praise

KNOW THAT THE LORD IS GOD. IT IS HE WHO MADE US, AND WE ARE HIS; WE ARE HIS PEOPLE, THE SHEEP OF HIS PASTURE. ENTER HIS GATES WITH THANKSGIVING AND HIS COURTS WITH PRAISE; GIVE THANKS TO HIM AND PRAISE HIS NAME. (PSALM 100:3-4)

R.I.O.T. — RIGHTEOUS INVASION OF TRUTH

Praise God. For what? You check the list. Below are lots of things worthy of a lift. Check every item and praise God for the gift:

- The beauty of creation.
- Friends.
- Family.
- Home.
- Church.
- Clothes.
- Joy.
- Parents.
- Teachers.
- Pastors and youth pastors.
- Wheels to drive.

- Job.
- Love.
- Life itself.
- Jesus' death on the cross.
- The indwelling Holy Spirit.
- The Father's love.
-

Other:_____

Now take this list. Stand up and shout! Yell your praises for each item you checked real loud from your mouth. Give God a standing ovation. Clap your hands in admiration! Let Him know it. Give Him a shout!

R.I.O.T. ACT

"It is good to praise the Lord and make music to your name, O Most High, to proclaim your love in the morning and your faithfulness at night." (Psalm 92:1-2)

Make a loud noise to Him who created the earth. Shake the rafters throughout the universe!

I Know There is a God

There is a hope
There is a light
There is an answer to all answers
There is a flame that burns in the night
And I know, I know, I know there is a God
There is a hope
There is a light
There is an answer to all answers
There is a flame that burns in the night
And I know, I know, I know there is a God
There is a God, there is a God
And I know, I know, I know there is a God

THE GOD WHO MADE THE WORLD AND EVERYTHING IN IT IS THE LORD OF HEAVEN AND EARTH AND DOES NOT LIVE IN TEMPLES BUILT BY HANDS.... FOR IN HIM WE LIVE AND MOVE AND HAVE OUR BEING. (ACTS 17:24,28)

R.I.O.T.—RIGHTEOUS INVASION OF TRUTH

What a mighty, glorious and wonderful God we serve! We rejoice in His creation. We enjoy everything we have and are at His hand. He provides us with air to breathe, water to drink, food to eat, clothes to wear, homes to live in and most of all, salvation for eternity. So where is the temple, where does the flame burn in the night?

It burns within us. We are the flame! We are His light. Jesus says, *"You are the light of the world."* (Matthew 5:14)

So where can you be the light and share with others the living God Who created the universe? First, share God the Creator with your family, your friends at school, and with those you know at church. Then, take Him to a lost and dying world! Help them look at the stars and see God's face. Help them know Him who created the human race!

R.I.O.T. ACT

"For you were once darkness, but now you are light in the Lord. Live as children of light." (Ephesians 5:8)

No need to fight and get all uptight. There is a God and you are a light! Praise the Lord for His creation and for giving you life!

Listen to My Story

Come on everybody
Listen to my story
Story about my Jesus
Amen, Amen
See the little baby
Lyin' in the manger
On Christmas morning
Amen, Amen

BUT THE ANGEL SAID TO THEM, "DO NOT BE AFRAID. I BRING YOU GOOD NEWS OF GREAT JOY THAT WILL BE FOR ALL THE PEOPLE. TODAY IN THE TOWN OF DAVID A SAVIOR HAS BEEN BORN TO YOU; HE IS CHRIST THE LORD." (LUKE 2:10,11)

R.I.O.T.—RIGHTEOUS INVASION OF TRUTH

ACT ONE

In a tiny town called Bethlehem, a young couple—Mary and Joseph—have a baby. The angel said to name Him Yeshua, meaning "God saves." This baby boy was special, let me tell you the story. Through Him God would offer salvation to all humanity. Within this baby boy was the hope of eternity.

This is a story about a life. The God-kind of LIFE! *"In him was life, and that life was the light of men." (John 1:4)* A choice for humanity had been made thousands of years before by Adam and Eve.

They chose knowledge over LIFE. So, LIFE was lost and death and sin reigned.

But God had a plan from before the foundation of the world to conquer death, and to bring life back to His battered man. This baby, Yeshua, was the plan.

So get ready for the story. We need to tell it again. About a baby who grew up to fully conquer sin. He was more than a man, He was God's only Son. He came to conquer Satan and give God's life to everyone.

R.I.O.T. ACT

"But when the time had fully come, God sent his Son, born of a woman, born under law, to redeem those under law, that we might receive the full rights of sons." (Galatians 4:4,5)

The only end to human strife is the LIFE. Proclaim Him this Christmas near the tree and lights!

Makin' Them Disciples

I can see Him by the seashore
Talkin' to those fishermen
He was makin' them disciples
Amen, Amen

AFTER THIS, JESUS WENT OUT AND SAW A TAX COLLECTOR BY THE NAME OF LEVI SITTING AT HIS TAX BOOTH. "FOLLOW ME," JESUS SAID TO HIM, AND LEVI GOT UP, LEFT EVERYTHING AND FOLLOWED HIM. (LUKE 5:27-28)

R.I.O.T. — RIGHTEOUS INVASION OF TRUTH

ACT TWO

After thirty years of preparation, Jesus is baptized in the Jordan, tempted in the wilderness and ready to begin His earthly ministry. Growing up close to the Sea of Galilee, Jesus begins to preach and heal throughout the region. Some fishermen first hear His message and heed His call. The call was simple, "Follow Me."

Jesus' message is also simple, "Repent for the Kingdom of God is at hand." But following isn't so simple. It means leaving job and family and walking the hills of Palestine for three years. Of course, those who follow don't know what's to come. They can't begin to imagine the coming miracles, signs, wonders and teaching they will experience through this One.

They will also be facing extreme criticism, attacks, persecution and threats on their lives. Still, twelve men respond to the call, "Follow Me." They lay down their lives and follow Jesus. They become disciples, as learners and followers of Jesus Christ.

What's in it for them? Certainly not fame, money or security. Some nights the only pillows they have are stones on the ground. The only covering they have are stars overhead. So, what's in it for them? Simple. LIFE. For the first time in history since Adam and Eve, LIFE walks the face of the earth. And they were there to see Him first. *"In Him was LIFE!" (John 1:4)*

R.I.O.T. ACT

Tired of mere existence? Living isn't LIFE until you've met Jesus. *"I have come that they may have LIFE, and have it to the full." (John 10:10)*

Jesus calls, Follow Me. When you follow, you'll be free!

Ridin' Through Jerusalem

Now He's ridin' through Jerusalem
Oh wave the palm branches
In pomp and splendor
Amen, Amen

WHEN HE CAME NEAR THE PLACE WHERE THE ROAD GOES DOWN THE MOUNT OF OLIVES, THE WHOLE CROWD OF DISCIPLES BEGAN JOYFULLY TO PRAISE GOD IN LOUD VOICES FOR ALL THE MIRACLES THEY HAD SEEN: "BLESSED IS THE KING WHO COMES IN THE NAME OF THE LORD!" (LUKE 19:37,38)

R.I.O.T.—RIGHTEOUS INVASION OF TRUTH

ACT THREE

After thirty years of preparation and three years of ministry, Jesus' life came down to one week of suffering. How difficult, how tough! Jesus came to die. He was LIFE and had never tasted sin, suffering or death. But in a few days, He would experience all three.

For now, the fickle crowd proclaimed Him king. In a few days, they would exclaim, "Crucify Him, blot out His name." Yes, He is the King, the Son of David. Yes, He deserved the crowds who followed and praised Him.

But what happened to the crowd when the parade was done? Would they still shout for Jesus at the end of their fun? Once the screamin' and cheerin' was over there was the cross and death to face. Some were only in it for the show, still Jesus knew and kept the pace. As for you, you must decide if following will last through the parade, as Satan tries to turn you out of Jesus' righteous way.

What will you do? Will you follow Him through the hills of Judea? Will you follow Him into Jerusalem?

R.I.O.T. ACT

Following Jesus goes beyond the crowd to the cross. *"Jesus said to them, 'You will indeed drink from my cup* [of suffering].'" *(Matthew 20:23)* Stick to the course, don't get lost.

After the parade, will your enthusiasm fade?

Prayin' to His Father

I can see Him in the garden
Prayin' to His Father
In deepest sorrow
Amen, Amen, Amen

HE WITHDREW ABOUT A STONE'S THROW BEYOND THEM, KNELT DOWN AND PRAYED, "FATHER, IF YOU ARE WILLING, TAKE THIS CUP FROM ME; YET NOT MY WILL, BUT YOURS BE DONE." (LUKE 22:41,42)

R.I.O.T.—RIGHTEOUS INVASION OF TRUTH

ACT FOUR

Jesus eats His last meal with the disciples in an upper room. Lifting up the bread, He tells them the bread is His body broken for them. Lifting up the cup of wine, He shares that the cup is His blood, shed for them on time. Confusion must have rushed through every disciple's mind except for one—Judas. He was the one who left to betray God's Son.

After the meal, the disciples and Jesus sing a special tune, then go to a favorite place to commune. The Garden of Gethsemane. Knowing the death He was to die, Jesus then prays to the Father on high. There is only one way:

His LIFE for our death;
His healing for disease;
His blood for our sins;
The cross of Jesus would give
God's life again.

But Jesus was also fully man—so He prayed to His Father for another plan. But there was no other, and Jesus resolved to take up His cross and die for all.

R.I.O.T. ACT

In the Garden, the only prayer to be prayed was, "Thy will, not mine be done." Jesus prayed that prayer for His life. Are you willing to pray that prayer for your life? *"I want to know Christ and the power of his resurrection and the fellowship of sharing in his sufferings, becoming like him in his death, and so, somehow, to attain to the resurrection of the dead." (Philippians 3:10-11)*

....

Each and every day learn more how to pray.

....

Led Before Pilate

Led before Pilate
His time had come to die
The crowds began to chant
Let Him be crucified

WITH ONE VOICE THEY CRIED OUT, "AWAY WITH THIS MAN! RELEASE BARABBAS TO US!..." WANTING TO RELEASE JESUS, PILATE APPEALED TO THEM AGAIN. BUT THEY KEPT SHOUTING, "CRUCIFY HIM! CRUCIFY HIM!" (LUKE 23:18,20-21)

R. I. O. T.—RIGHTEOUS INVASION OF TRUTH

ACT FIVE

The Jewish leaders held a mock trial and demanded that the Romans crucify Jesus. Herod and Pilate were both unconvinced of any crime that Jesus may have committed. Still, the crowds had turned on Jesus. In that day, many Jews were hoping the Messiah would come as a military leader to drive the Romans out of the land, and Jesus didn't fit the bill. So the only thing left to do was to catch Him and kill.

Jesus doesn't always fulfill our expectations either. If we always had our way, He would sometimes be holy, and other times play.

Would you crucify Jesus if He didn't do what you wanted Him to? Think about it. The Bible says it is even possible to crucify Jesus again in open

110

shame if we choose to walk away from Him (Hebrews 6:6). True, that would be totally extreme. But the Bible says it's possible all the same.

Also, whenever we hurt another person, we put a nail into His Hand. Whenever we hate and turn our back on someone needy, we yell "crucify Him!" again. How? By rejecting Jesus' love and sacrifice for others, His work on the cross goes unnoticed by others.

R.I.O.T. ACT

"I have been crucified with Christ and I no longer live, but Christ lives in me." (*Galatians 2:20*)

So, don't yell, "Crucify Him" again and again. Instead, cry out, "I'm saved, I'm saved in Him!"

It Is Finished

They nailed Him to a cross
It is finished He had said

WHEN HE HAD RECEIVED THE DRINK, JESUS SAID, "IT IS FINISHED." (JOHN 19:30)

R.I.O.T.—RIGHTEOUS INVASION OF TRUTH

ACT SIX

It is finished.
    So, what's finished?
Death's finished, so is sin and grief.
It is finished.
    So, what's finished?
Reconciliation and redemption we've been
    given holy relief.
It is finished.
        Jesus' ministry on earth and God's
            loving plan.
To give,
        Everyone in bondage a new heart—
            new man!
Finished. It is finished. Jesus broke every
    chain,
        He healed every heart,
            And restored the lame.
Have you heard the eternal cry, "It is finished"
    today?
        Are you free?

Are you saved?
If not, simply say—
It is finished, Jesus save me, help me finish today.

R.I.O.T. ACT

"Now if we died with Christ, we believe that we will also live with him." (Romans 6:8)

The cry of every heart's wish is to hear Him say, "It is finished. Well done thy good and faithful servant."

The Lamb of God

Then in a borrowed tomb
The Lamb of God lay dead

THE WOMEN WHO HAD COME WITH JESUS FROM GALILEE FOLLOWED JOSEPH AND SAW THE TOMB AND HOW HIS BODY WAS LAID IN IT. THEN THEY WENT HOME AND PREPARED SPICES AND PERFUMES. (LUKE 23:55-56)

R.I.O.T. — RIGHTEOUS INVASION OF TRUTH

ACT SEVEN

It's Friday,
> Jesus is on the cross dyin',
> All the women gathered around are cryin'.

It's Friday,
> Devil's thinking he's won,
> Clouds are blockin' out the sun.

It's Friday,
> Romans gamble over His clothes,
> A sword in His side deals the final blow.

It's Friday,
> It's really very sad,
> On either side of Jesus dies a man who's been real bad.

It's Friday,

Pharisees and Sadducees rejoice at
their plot,
The disciples flee in fear, there's
nothing they can stop.

It's Friday,
All they'd hoped for seem to be lost,
Every hope seemed to die upon that
rugged cross.

It's Friday,
Jesus dies and is buried in the
tomb,
But God's not finished, don't sing that
final tune.

It's Friday,
The devil's really finished, never
count God out,
'Cause Sunday mornin's comin' and
all heaven's gonna shout!

R.I.O.T. ACT

"Where, O death, is your victory? Where, O death, is your sting?" (1 Corinthians 15:55)

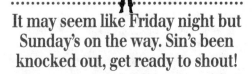

It may seem like Friday night but Sunday's on the way. Sin's been knocked out, get ready to shout!

Early Sunday Mornin'

But then early Sunday mornin'
I said early Sunday mornin'

ON THE FIRST DAY OF THE WEEK, VERY EARLY IN THE MORNING, THE WOMEN TOOK THE SPICES THEY HAD PREPARED AND WENT TO THE TOMB. THEY FOUND THE STONE ROLLED AWAY FROM THE TOMB. (LUKE 24:1-2)

R.I.O.T.—RIGHTEOUS INVASION OF TRUTH

ACT EIGHT

Resurrection day was a day of new LIFE. The tomb was empty, the woman found, and living would never again be bound.

In that tomb they found only His graveclothes. His body was missing and the Romans were hissing. But the ladies were praising for Jesus Christ's raising!

Think about it. Even though Jesus has been raised from the dead, at times we try to slip His graveclothes back over our head! We drag out past sin, guilt and pain instead of leaving it where we left it to wear it again.

Imagine how stinky a dead body would be if we dug it up now. Got the picture?

Pee-yuu and how! Once you surrender your life to Jesus, you are dead and buried in Him. No reason at all to drag out those graveclothes and put them on again. Get it?

"What shall we say, then? Shall we go on sinning so that grace may increase? By no means! We died to sin; how can we live in it any longer?" (Romans 6:1-2)

R.I.O.T. ACT

"Therefore, there is now no condemnation for those who are in Christ Jesus." (Romans 8:1)

Don't dig up the past. You're free at last!

He Arose!

Just before the sun
Came over the eastern sky
The trees began to rattle
And the birds began to fly
And the earth started to rumble
And the stone was rolled away
Then Jesus Christ, the Son of God
He arose, He arose, He arose
He walked alive out of the grave!

WHY DO YOU LOOK FOR THE LIVING AMONG THE DEAD? HE IS NOT HERE; HE HAS RISEN! (LUKE 24:5-6)

R. I. O. T. — RIGHTEOUS INVASION OF TRUTH

ACT NINE

The devil was having a party late on Saturday night. Some of the demons were out of it, some were drunk and ugly uptight. A few got into fights but most were simply down. Then suddenly the gates shook and an earthquake shook the ground. Light appeared where darkness for eons shrouded light and sound. Blinded by the light and cowering in fear, the devil looked up and behold, who should appear?

Jesus stood there looking nothing like He did before. Clothed in glory He carried a huge sword through the devil's deadly door. Like deafening thunder, His voice came through the cloud, "The keys, O fallen one, give them to Me now." Then without any resistance, the keys to death and hell flew into Jesus' hands. His authority broke every bondage as Satan turned and ran.

No longer did the devil have the right to sin and death. Jesus' blood had been shed and death's power was finally dead. Then as suddenly as He appeared, He was back on earth. It was Sunday morning and the faithful, would soon proclaim His worth.

R.I.O.T. ACT

Claim it. It's real. He is risen! *"But Christ has indeed been raised from the dead, the firstfruits of those who have fallen asleep." (1 Corinthians 15:20)*

You're released from hell's prison 'cause Jesus is risen!

Everybody Said Praise Him!

*And everybody said
Somebody praise Him, say
Say it over now
Amen, Amen*

I WANT TO KNOW CHRIST AND THE POWER OF HIS RESURRECTION.... (PHILIPPIANS 3:10)

R.I.O.T.—RIGHTEOUS INVASION OF TRUTH

Why praise Him? Let's think of all the reasons:

- Jesus paid the penalty of sin on the cross for us.
- Jesus defeated the devil.
- Jesus gave us LIFE.
- Jesus lifted us up into heavenly places.
- Jesus healed our diseases.
- Jesus broke our bondages.
- Jesus purified us with His blood.
- Jesus made us holy—He sent His Holy Spirit.
- Jesus defeated sin and death.
- Jesus gave us His life.
- Jesus reconciled us to God.
- Jesus showed us the true meaning of love.
- Jesus started the Church and made us part of His family.
- Jesus gave us power to live in the truth and to be free.

Now you list at least five more things the risen Jesus has done for you:

1.
2.
3.
4.
5.

R.I.O.T. ACT

"But you are a chosen people, a royal priesthood, a holy nation, a people belonging to God, that you may declare the praises of him who called you out of darkness into his wonderful light." (1 Peter 2:9)

....

Praise Him for His resurrection! Praise Him for your new direction!

....

It's a Celebration

Lift your voice and sing
It's a celebration
It's the resurrection
Amen, Amen
Oh yeah
Give Him glory

THEY WILL CELEBRATE YOUR ABUNDANT GOODNESS AND JOYFULLY SING OF YOUR RIGHTEOUSNESS. (PSALM 145:7)

R.I.O.T.—RIGHTEOUS INVASION OF TRUTH

What do you celebrate?
  Beating your big high school rival in
    anything? Yes!
Having that special person say "yes" to the first
    date? Yes!
  Getting your driver's license? Yes!
Getting a new car to go with your license? Yes!
  Lettering in a varsity sport? Yes!
Getting all the highest marks from the judges
    in state band or orchestra or choir?
    Yes!
Someone you love has a birthday or gets
    married? Yes!
Someone you love accepts Jesus as Lord and
    Savior? Yes!
What are some of most recent celebrations you

have had in your life?

Most celebrations in the world only last for a season. A team wins the super bowl, and the next season they have to start over again. But some celebrations last longer like a new baby being born, a wedding, and most of all, being saved in Jesus. That's one celebration that doesn't end. An end of sin get's the celebration to begin—but its end is eternal—it never ends!

The most exciting event in all of history worth celebrating is the resurrection of Jesus Christ. Hiding because of fear behind closed doors, the disciples thought it was over when Pilate put Jesus on the cross. But two days later He walked through their door! The apostle Paul tells us in 1 Corinthians 15, that Jesus appeared to over 500 more! And He is still appearing to those like you who have chosen to seek Him. He is risen from the dead—never stop praisin'!

R.I.O.T. ACT

"Rejoice in the Lord always. I will say it again: Rejoice!" (Philippians 4:4)

Get rid of that frown. Satan's come down. Celebrate! God is great!

Worthy to be Praised!

God is worthy
Amen
He's alive
He's alive
And He's worthy to be praised
Amen

WORTHY IS THE LAMB, WHO WAS SLAIN, TO RECEIVE POWER AND WEALTH AND WISDOM AND STRENGTH AND HONOR AND GLORY AND PRAISE! (REVELATION 5:12)

R.I.O.T.—RIGHTEOUS INVASION OF TRUTH

Jesus has been raised. Give Him praise! From before the foundation of the world, Jesus knew that He'd give His life for you. Now you have the privilege of living a new life in Christ with a brand new identity, a new name and new authority to take back what the devil has taken from you.

So, get ready to give Him praise for who you are in Him:

Say it now with praise with a big grin...

      I am a saint.

I am saved.

      I am royalty.

I am a new creation.

I am holy.